D1484398

RIVER

Poems by
Peggy Trojan

River copyright © 2020 by Peggy Trojan

All rights reserved.

Except for quotations and excerpts appearing in reviews, this work may not be reproduced or transmitted, in whole or in part, by any means whatsoever, without prior written permission from the author.

ISBN: 9798564539234

Cover photo and design by Kari Jensen

Copies of this book are available on *amazon.com*

For Dave

CONTENTS

Winter Poem

When the gray of the city
chokes the winter sun
and commitments weigh
like deadlines on your mind,
when rushing street people
look confused by their sadness,
the too familiar air
hard to breathe,

Remember the river,
exuberant and giddy,
the deep forest, forever inviting.
Listen, in the distance,
the beating of the drum.

Poem for Dave

I found you
when I was young,
walking fast,
laughing eyes,
shallow guise,
tight with swagger
and invitation.

I find you now
life almost spent
walking slow,
no special place to go,
years wise,
knowing eyes,
still learning
love is always
indefinitely perfect.

At the Controls

Starts it up, puts it in autopilot,
takes his foot off the gas.
Relaxes. Surveys the countryside.
Marine helicopters, twenty years,
taught him to scan.
"See that Cooper's Hawk, two o'clock high?"

Makes a check of cloud formation.
"That cumulus topping off? Rain."
The roar of cement corduroy
beyond the white line
startles him back into his lane.
Checks his instruments,
readjusts his thinking.
Accepts input from his co-pilot.
"Stop sign!" "Post office."

Domestic list finished,
heads home,
mission accomplished.
Makes a perfect landing
up the runway and into the garage.

Lessons

When this life is done
and accountings given
for lessons learned of love,
let all hear
I learned the most
those many times
you loved me
when I could not
love myself.

Honestly

If you are not truthful
I am reduced
to a non-person
and you can act
without reaction.
If you are not truthful
you will never know
who I am.

Alone

Sometimes, alone at night,
when fears spring out from dark,
I speak love for you aloud
(words, whole rambling sentences)
to test their meaning.
To listen
for some echoing response.

In the quiet
familiar bed,
I remember
the poems of your hands.

Partnered

Remember when we first shared bed,
skin hungry, pasted together
belly to belly?
Breathing the hot used air,
letting our limbs go numb,
we thought we could sleep
like that forever.

Now we share gold years and bed,
quiet on our own claimed side,
space between our weighted backs.
Breathing our own wide air,
we move often
to adjust blood and dreams.

When I sense your body sighing,
surrendering to sleep,
I slide my foot across the smooth divide
to touch your leg for anchor.

New Sheets

Sleep peacefully
in this bed of flowers,
feel spring turn gray to green
and everything new
when birds, trees
and most people
get a chance
to bloom again
with astounding
vigor.

Sleep soundly among these
printed blooms
and feel my multi-colored love.

Early Light

In the morning,
when the world first
becomes reality
and you move beside me
in the effort of waking,
I savor the warmth
of your touch
before you are aware
you are touching,
and love's quiet energy
flows through me
like wind in trees,
leaving small parts
still quivering slightly
when the radio clicks on.

Routine

This morning
the glow of your kiss
is still on my smile
as I watch you
make your way down the street
in our own recognizable pattern.
This morning
the warmth of your body
is still on my skin
and I am happy
because I love you.

Marriage Stock Report

Having invested all my savings
in an unproved company,
choosing carefully
yet banking on luck,
and having ridden
the ups and downs of years,
taken losses and gains,
resisted the chance
to sell at market crash,
believing and looking
for long-term growth,

I am now reaping
the rewards of my investment.
My portfolio is worth
many times what I paid.
Diversified, multiplied, secure.
The interest compounds daily,
making me in old age
wealthy beyond dreams.

Assurance

Long stemmed roses
nestled in white tissue
brought to the door
by the florist
or dipped milk chocolates
and a flowery card
extolling your undying love
was accepted proof
when we were young.
Now, in our twilight,
warming my side
of the winter bed
works as well,
as does coffee perking
in the morning.

After Sauna

We came from sauna,
reddened, sweating,
ready for cool down.
Dave suggested
we sit on the deck
in the dark summer night
in the rain,
stark naked
there in our woods.

Adjusting my bulk
to the unfamiliar webbing,
I laughed
at our impudence,
felt young,
strong and naughty.
Then, sat back,
and shamelessly
lifted my face
to the rain.

Heading Out

I'll be leaving soon.
    Oh, where are you going?
Heading north I think.
    Well don't go into the lake.
I won't.
    Have you packed a suitcase?
I won't need one.
    Do you have any money?
I won't need that either.
    How are you traveling?
A bus will pick me up on the road.
    How will you know where to get off?
The driver will tell me.
    Can I come with you?
Not yet.

Death Do Us Part

When we were young and eager
we promised to stay together until death.
We could not imagine a disease
called Lewy body dementia would
over years destroy everything.

First forgetting facts, dates,
names, where you were going,
movies, books, conversation,
how to play piano, then flying,
driving.

And now the devastating loss
of balance. You fall
over and over, inside,
outside, even holding the deck rail.

You say, "I feel lost."
I answer, "Me too."

Shower

I add showers
to my caretaking,
help you undress
and into the new chair.
Adjust water temperature,
hand you soap and cloth,
scrub your back,
rinse you off,
help you dry and dress.

I remember when
watching you disrobe
could spark a fire.

First Night

I leave you at Memory Care.
Trust a bevy of staffers
in their twenties
to cope with your waking,
your walking, your falling,
your dreaming.

Tonight we sleep alone.
I miss your hand
reaching for me in the dark.

Shirts

I chose your shirts carefully
when I packed for Memory Care,
wanting you to look good.
I bought permanent press plaids,
no need to iron.

Today I go back home.
In the closet,
faded denims, winter wools,
that mosquito repellent one,
my favorite brown and white linen,
summer polos, chamois, corduroys,
shirts I sewed for Christmas.
None you will ever wear again.

I gather them all in a bear hug,
bury my face in your old
Black Watch flannel
and weep.

Traveler

You traveled the world,
often taking a different route
just for fun.
Backpacked with me
in Honduras and Guatemala.
Toured Germany, France,
the Netherlands.
Taught college in Japan, Mexico.
Visited my relatives in Finland.
Took our six children
to almost every state and Canada.

Now you are confined
to a building where you
walk the halls, need assistance
to find your room.

Walker

You were safe during my visits.
In my absence, nineteen falls
in five months. Stitches
in your leg, bandaged elbows,
fractured wrist, ankle,
staples in your head,
black and blue from armpit
to groin. Finally broken ribs
and punctured lung
sent you to the hospital
and into a wheelchair.

Whenever you fell,
you called my name.

Lunch at Memory Care

The men choose to sit together
at the big table covered in white linen.
From different backgrounds,
teachers, managers, owners,
farmers, professors, military men,
fathers, grandfathers.
Sharing no history, no futures,
they have nothing to talk about.

With good men of like mind,
you quietly wait to be served.

Where We Live

You did not question the changes,
did not ask why we moved your chair,
photos of family and planes,
your clothes in new closets.
Never objected to living
at Memory Care.

One day you asked,
"Where do you live now?"
I answered, "Close by.
I'll see you tomorrow,"
kissed you goodbye.

How could I explain
to make you understand?
Decades ago I staked a claim
of memories and love.
Maintained it, updated it,
repaired it when damaged.
I live at my homestead
in your heart.

Secrets

Over the years
as we trusted more,
we shared secrets,
sure they were safe.
I promise to keep them
while you blissfully
forget them all.

Outing

We thought it was a good idea
to sign you out of their care,
take you for a ride
through the park
along the river.
Autumn leaves brilliant.
You fell asleep in half a mile.

In the sixties
when the girls were babies,
gas twenty-nine cents a gallon,
we drove around until they slept.

I wanted to pick you up,
carry you to bed,
tuck you in
and kiss the top of your head
without waking you.

Social Distance

Because of COVID-19
we are forced to visit
through the window,
make short calls on FaceTime
which you do not understand.

What is hard,
what breaks my heart,
is social distancing with you.
I need to be with you,
to touch you,
to remind you who I am.
You need the same,
saying in your confusion,
"I just want you to come home."

Together

We transfer you
into the small apartment
I had rented on the river,
filled with furniture
and art from home.
Every item familiar.
Daughter Mary moves in.

You nap on the couch,
your head on my shoulder.
We are happy, hold hands
like young lovers.
Presence heals us.
When I kiss you,
we smile.

Welcome Home

Twenty-eight pounds thinner,
you did not eat or talk.
It appeared you had forgotten
how to chew and swallow.
We tried smoothies, juice, soup,
every meal a concern.

One day Bill,
a colleague and friend
for fifty years,
baked you a pie.
Cherry pie, your favorite.
Huge with an impressive
latticed crust.

We watched amazed
as you ate bite after bite,
feeding body
and spirit.

Simple Joys

On the balcony
with sun and birds,
you are more talkative.
"This is a new heaven."

Your sense of humor is back,
you thank us for our efforts.
"Mary, you're a peach."

We watch Packers, Brewers,
fishing, Planet Earth.
"I saw this one before."
Listen to Brahms and Beethoven.
Share daily photos with family.

We wheel you
on downtown river walks.
You wave at kayakers
from the bridge,
greet dogs we pass,
eat takeout in the park.
Find our way to Olson's for a cone.
"Strawberry, of course."

One day from across the living room
you announce,
"Peggy, I'm still nuts about you!"

Four months,
every day a gift.

Duty

Sometimes you talk in your sleep,
back years, at the air base
where you have not been
for decades.
Insist you need to report for duty.

I hope your buddies
are waiting for you,
your helicopter
warmed up
and ready to go.

Destination

You died as you lived.
No complaints, no demands.
Quietly at home
with Mary and me,
whispering my name.
Kids phoned goodbye,
we held hands.
Focused, ready for adventure,
eyes open to see
where you were going.

Always

Good night.
Sleep well.
I love you.
I'll see you
in the morning.

River

Stay on the river now,
it will lead you to the sea.
Someday I will meet you there
with all those we have loved.

Listen, can you hear?
                    The river is singing.

ACKNOWLEDGMENTS

The following poems have previously appeared either in print or online:

"After Sauna." *Symmetry, Talking Stick 23* (2014); *Essence.* Portage Press, 2015.

"Alone." *All that Matters* (2018).

"Assurance." *All that Matters* (2018).

"At the Controls." *All that Matters* (2018).

"Early Light." *Red Cedar* (2015).

"Honestly." *All that Matters* (2018).

"Lessons." *Eye on Life Magazine* (2012); *Red Cedar* (2012).

"New Sheets." *All that Matters* (2018).

"Partnered." *Dust & Fire* (2011); *RAV'N* (2012); *Golden Words, Wisconsin Senior Poet Laureate* (2012); *Your Daily Poem* Feb. 13, 2013.

"Poem for Dave." *We Are Poetry* (2015).

"Routine." *All that Matters* (2018).

"Winter Poem." *Essence.* Portage Press, 2015.

ABOUT THE AUTHOR

Peggy Trojan published her first poem in 2010 when she was seventy-seven and has since been published in a wide variety of journals and anthologies.

Peggy's first chapbook *Everyday Love*, a collection of poems about her parents, placed second in the Wisconsin Fellowship of Poets chapbook contest in 2015 and was a finalist for the Northeast Minnesota Book Awards. Her chapbook *Homefront: Childhood Memories of WWII* was published by Evening Street Press. Peggy's full-length collection *Essence* won publication by Portage Press. Her third chapbook *Free Range Kids*, published by Evening Street Press, won the Helen Kay Chapbook Contest. In 2018, Peggy compiled her poems into a 236-page book called *All that Matters* so her family and friends would have most of her work in one book.

In *River*, Peggy Trojan's life of growing old with her husband David are suddenly interrupted by his diagnosis of Lewy body dementia.* Through her sparse, honest poems, she takes us from the joys of sharing a bed to the heartbreak of watching her talented, intelligent husband reduced to depending on others for care. David passed away in September 2020. Peggy spends her time between her apartment on the Chippewa River in Eau Claire and the home she built with David in the woods near Brule, Wisconsin.

*Lewy body dementia (LBD) is the second most common form of progressive dementia after Alzheimer's.

Made in the USA
Monee, IL
07 June 2021

69494958R00028